A gift from:

_____

To:

_____

The plans of the LORD stand firm.

Psalm 33:11

God Always Has a Plan B
Copyright © 1999 by The Zondervan Corporation
ISBN-10: 0-310-81191-0
ISBN-13: 978-0-310-81191-6

Developed in association with Women of Faith, 1-888-49-FAITH.
Scripture taken from the Holy Bible: New International Version™
(North American Edition). Copyright 1973, 1978, 1984, by
International Bible Society. Used by permission of Zondervan. All
rights reserved.

NIV and *New International Version* trademarks are registered in the
United States Patent and Trademark Office by International Bible
Society.

Requests for information should be addressed to:
Inspirio, the gift group of Zondervan
Grand Rapids, MI 49530

Project Manager: Tom Dean
Production Manager: Matt Nolan
Design Manager: Michael J. Williams
Illustrations: Tom LaBaff, www.tomlabaff.com
Design: Michael J. Williams

Printed in China
06 07 08 / 5 4 3 2 1

God Always Has a Plan B

inspirio®

When I said, "My foot is slipping,"
    your love, O LORD, supported me.
When anxiety was great within me,
    your consolation brought joy to my soul.
The LORD has become my fortress,
    and my God the rock in whom I take refuge.

Psalm 94:18–19, 22

He will fill your mouth with laughter
    and your lips with shouts of joy.
Your enemies will be clothed in shame,
    and the tents of the wicked will be no more.

Job 8:21–22

*The Spirit helps us in our weakness. We do not
know what we ought to pray for, but the Spirit
himself intercedes for us with groans that
words cannot express.*

Romans 8:26

A reporter stood in front of a fire as it consumed a house, and then he turned to see the homeowners and their little son watching it burn. The reporter, fishing for a human-interest angle, said to the boy, "Son, it looks as if you don't have a home anymore." The little boy promptly answered, "Oh, yes, we have a home. We just don't have a house to put it in."

Barbara Johnson

When children are secure, they feel free to be who they really are. That's how you and I can live too. God is the only one who knows everything about us. He knows our good thoughts and the thoughts that we struggle to admit even to ourselves. So no matter what you could tell someone else about your life that would change that person's opinion of you, nothing you could say would dampen God's heart toward you. He knows it all, and he loves you. Surely, this kind of security should set us free to be who we really are.

Sheila Walsh

God Always Has a Plan B

Let the Lord have his complete way with you. He loves you so much and has far greater plans for you than you can ever have for yourself. And he does make everything beautiful in his time. Allow God to move in you powerfully. Yield to his voice—calling deeper—higher still. He will take you there.

Kathy Troccoli

One of the most wonderful aspects of our relationship with Christ is that we don't have to talk—he understands. When you are in pain, it is so exhausting to have to try and explain to others what you are feeling. What a relief it is to be able to lie down in a field with the Shepherd and not have to say a word.

Sheila Walsh

When a sudden ray of sun or a moonbeam falls
on a dreary street, it makes no difference what it
illumines—a broken bottle on the ground, a fading
flower in a field, or the flaxen blonde hair of a child's
head. The object is transformed and the viewer is
transfixed. Celebrate that moment of beauty, and take it
with you in your memory. It is God's gift to you.

Luci Swindoll

Laughter is a riotous vote of acceptance that God is the
God-who-sees. Whatever it is probably won't go away,
so we might as well live and laugh through it. When we
double over laughing, we're bending so we won't break.
If you think your particular troubles are too heavy and
too traumatic to laugh about, remember that laughing
is like changing a baby's diaper. It doesn't solve any
problems permanently, but it makes things more
acceptable for awhile.

Barbara Johnson

So often we kick and scream at the thought of yielding. We don't want to give up control. If we could just understand that yielding to a benevolent and trustworthy "other" can bring quietness, rest, and even happiness.

It isn't just babies who resist yielding. And it isn't just those whose minds are tormented and distrustful. It's all of us who for various reasons can't or won't trust in the promise of rest that yielding offers.

When I find I am unable to yield a point or to yield to the spirit of Jesus, I ask myself: What am I holding on to? Why is it so difficult to simply yield, knowing full well that I will benefit from doing so? God promises to work in me and in my will. Since in my humanness I have trouble letting go and yielding, I'm enormously comforted by this promise of his active work in my will.

Marilyn Meberg

Thanks be to God, who always leads us in triumphal procession in Christ and through us spreads everywhere the fragrance of the knowledge of him.

2 Corinthians 2:14

May he give you the desire of your heart
  and make all your plans succeed.
We will shout for joy when you are victorious
  and will lift up our banners in the name of
  our God.
May the LORD grant all your requests.

Psalm 20:4–5

God Always Has a Plan B

The issue of cleanliness on this polluted planet is a constant one. Every day we shower, scrub, scrape, soak, and scour in an attempt to stay healthy and socially acceptable. In fact, I have a basket at my tub side filled with cleaning utensils: sponges, brushes, pumices, and soaps. As helpful as these items are, they do not compare to how clean I feel when I have spent moments in the Lord's presence. I am cleansed in the innermost parts of my being where even the sauna's steam can't penetrate.

Patsy Clairmont

Years ago a friend of mine offered to share her daylilies with me. I observed there were whole stalks of buds and that God's plan was that when one conked out—finished for the day—another one (or two) would open up. I pondered the thought that God felt it was worth it to create one flower to bloom for one day. If a lily is worth it, I'm worth it! That thought empowered me to go on when it would have been easy to give up.

Sue Buchanan

When life becomes especially hard and troubles seem to gang up on us, I have a few suggestions.

Don't struggle and fret and try to cope all by yourself. Put the situation in God's hands, trusting that he will bring it to the conclusion that is best for everyone involved.

Pray for guidance and believe that direction is being given to you now.

Pray for and practice a calm attitude.

Let faith saturate your thoughts.

Remind yourself of one great truth: Hard experiences do pass. They will yield. So just hold on, with God's help.

Remember that there is always a light in the darkness. Believe that and look for it; it is the light of God's love.

Ask the Lord to release your ingenuity so that you can face the problem creatively with strength and wisdom.

Remember that others experience troubles similar to yours. Our heavenly Father is committed to shaping us into his image, and so he knows the ultimate value of each painful experience. No, traumas are not unique—to you or to this time in history. The road sign has marked everyone's path. God asks us to face these dead ends with an air of expectancy that his peace and power will prevail. And they will.

Barbara Johnson

The LORD is my strength and my shield;
    my heart trusts in him, and I am helped.
My heart leaps for joy
    and I will give thanks to him in song.

Psalm 28:7

I am God, and there is no other;
    I am God, and there is none like me.
What I have said, that will I bring about;
    what I have planned, that will I do.

Isaiah 46:9, 11

Commit to the LORD whatever you do,
    and your plans will succeed.

Proverbs 16:3

Be joyful at your Feast — you, your sons and daughters.... For the LORD your God will bless you in all your harvest and in all the work of your hands, and your joy will be complete.

Deuteronomy 16:14–15

Is anything too hard for the LORD?

Genesis 18:14

God had planned something better for us so that only together with us would they be made perfect.

Hebrews 11:40

Lord, make me increasingly aware that to be chosen by You also includes Your choices of those who nurture me in ways too many and magnificent for me to imagine. The feast at which I am sitting is more luxurious than I can comprehend. My simple table blessing is inadequate, but ... thank you!

Joy MacKenzie

One of the things I find fascinating about God's creation is the way he seems to temper the negative environmental elements with corresponding positive ones. For instance, without the nearly ceaseless rains of the Northwest, no incomparable green scenery would greet the eye from all directions. God's creative style ensures that something wonderful will offset something less than wonderful. In everything, God seems so balanced. I love that about him.

Marilyn Meberg

My driver, Shooter, once told me, "The sun comes up every morning, and I'm grateful for another day to be alive. And you know what? If the sun never came up, we could all use a flashlight." His words touched me deeply. I am a believer in Jesus and his promises: If the sun doesn't shine I do indeed have a flashlight—his Word. I can hold out my flashlight, enabling others to see and be comforted when the sun is not shining and the days are like nights.

Kathy Troccoli

If we can, with our limited visibility, see the humor in a situation, even if it's tucked off in a corner, we will find our path is an easier one.

Barbara Johnson

My life philosophy in a nutshell is "Life is tough, but God is faithful."

Sheila Walsh

If you're a parent, pain is inevitable, but misery is optional. As the saying goes, even the sun has a sinking spell every evening. But the next morning, like bread dough in the darkness of the oven, it rises. We Christian parents can hit bottom just like anyone else. But we have a special ability that nonbelievers don't have. We bounce! So when you feel yourself plummeting into the closet, be sure to leave the door open. That way you won't knock it down on your way out.

Barbara Johnson

Myrtle Pate made everything more fun. As I have matured, her presence in my life has remained important wherever life has taken us. I have drawn courage and strength from this gentle, yet strong, woman. Her life confirms what she taught me as a young girl so many years ago — we can put our trust in a sovereign God. We can count on his presence as we learn life's lessons — and press on.

Peggy Benson

If your love is for the left lane, swing on over there and feel the wind flying through your hair and the bugs spatting against your dark glasses. But if the right lane beckons you, indulge your penchant for counting wildflowers in the field or discarded tennis shoes on the freeway. Most important, we must all remember, left-laners or right-laners, we are to be tender with each other.

Marilyn Meberg

The story is told of a terrible fire on a farm that wiped out everything the farmer owned. When the flames had died down, the farmer walked sadly through the smoldering mass of all that was left of his life's work. His boot caught the charred body of a hen. When he turned it over, he discovered tiny, peeping chicks, alive and well under the body of their mother. She had given her life to protect her young. To me a mother's love is a God-given gift, a glimpse of heaven, a picture seen through smoky glass of how passionately God's heart beats for us.

Sheila Walsh

God Always Has a Plan B

I don't know the circumstances of your life. Maybe you have health problems. Maybe you're experiencing a financial crisis, a relational struggle, or a genuine feeling of inadequacy. Whatever your biggest problems, be sure you aren't surrendering to the odds. You may look at yourself and say, "I can't. I can't rise above this, get beyond it, or overcome," and so you give up. Let me say with all the love in the world, my friend, don't quit. You're just starting this ride. You have the whole sky above your head. God wants to free you from bondage, and he knows just how to do it.

Luci Swindoll

Laughter is the language of the young at heart and the antidote to what ails us. No drugstore prescription is required; laughter is available to anyone at any time. Laughter's benefits are felt immediately. With large doses, the benefits show on our face, in our body language, and in the spring in our step. God gave us this capacity to be tickled way deep down inside. Giggles are as contagious as a viral disease. And you know what? You don't have to be happy to laugh. You become happy because you laugh.

Barbara Johnson

It seems that our tendency, if we are strong, is to err toward abrasiveness, which diminishes our strength and hardens the shoulder we have to offer a hurting world. Who wants to rest her head against a brick wall? Ouch!

When I'm bewildered and overwhelmed, I seek the gentle guidance of a person I know will respond with compassion. Life is complicated enough without having to listen to the caustic remarks of someone's misdirected strength.

I would love to tell you that I first run to the Lord for a shoulder to cry on, to bolster my courage, and to find a balm for my bruised soul. But sometimes I am negligent, until all my other options are depleted. Then I remember. Gratefully, I know it is his plan that we extend ourselves to one another. Certainly not in place of him, but as a way to be honorably connected to each other through him.

Patsy Clairmont

I can usually spot a rut-dweller from twenty paces (takes
one to know one). They lack luster, imagination, energy,
and interest. They tend to slurp, slump, and sleep a lot.
They prefer to gripe rather than grow, and they enjoy
whine with their candlelight. Who really wants to be like
that? Now just imagine what might happen if we were
to step out of our old routine and deliberately walk in
his ways. Why, we might even do a little break dancing
on our way up and out of that hard place. C'mon, rut-
dwellers, boogie out of there. Risk life!

Patsy Clairmont

Difficulties are opportunities for growth. How can we
grow with no problems? The world is watching how the
Christian acts under pressure. So don't be a pressure-
filled bottle, but allow God to make something out of
your problem. If we can stop complaining, we can start
proclaiming what God is doing through our difficulties.
Find a support group. And remind yourself that after
every Calvary comes an Easter.

Barbara Johnson

Sing, O Daughter of Zion;
*   shout aloud, O Israel!*
Be glad and rejoice with all your heart,
*   O Daughter of Jerusalem!*
The LORD your God is with you,
*   he is mighty to save.*
He will take great delight in you,
*   he will quiet you with his love,*
*   he will rejoice over you with singing.*

Zephaniah 3:14, 17

Sing to the LORD, you saints of his;
*   praise his holy name.*
For his anger lasts only a moment,
*   but his favor lasts a lifetime;*
weeping may remain for a night,
*   but rejoicing comes in the morning.*

Psalm 30:4–5

Don't ever forget the place you have with Jesus. It is a place that is reserved for you and you alone—so close to his heart that on some days if you close your eyes and listen intently, you may hear his very breath. It is his breath that continually breathes life into your soul. You are so deeply loved. Walk arm in arm with him today. Your eternal escort. Your faithful bridegroom. He will never let you go.

Kathy Troccoli

Someone said, "Our glory is not in never falling, but in rising each time we fall." I believe the secret of success is to stay cool and calm on top and pedal like crazy underneath. When you do fall and skin your knees, get up again and start all over under the impetus of the Holy Spirit. Stay in the race. Find your pace, then shift into cruise gear. Use the momentum!

Barbara Johnson

I will praise the LORD, *who counsels me;*
    even at night my heart instructs me.
You have made known to me the path of life;
    you will fill me with joy in your presence,
    with eternal pleasures at your right hand.

Psalm 16:7, 11

In his heart a man plans his course,
    but the LORD *determines his steps.*

Proverbs 16:9

Do not fear, for I am with you;
    do not be dismayed, for I am your God.
I will strengthen you and help you;
    I will uphold you with my righteous right
    hand.

Isaiah 41:10

God Always Has a Plan B

Jason climbed into his mother's arms. I watched this small boy's face as he looked at his mother. He seemed so content, so safe, so cared for. I asked Jason what he loved about her. His five-year-old heart quickly responded, "She's my friend." He thought a little more, then, "She's my hero." Finally, with a deep sigh, he said, "She's my everything." His mother hugged and kissed him, and I was reminded of the many, many times I have felt content and safe in the arms of Jesus, trusting my life, my concerns, and my hopes into his care.

He longs to hold you, to care for you. He longs to meet your needs and for you to put your trust in him. He is a faithful God with arms that will never let you go.

Kathy Troccoli

You crown the year with your bounty,
and your carts overflow with abundance.
The grasslands of the desert overflow;
the hills are clothed with gladness.
The meadows are covered with flocks
and the valleys are mantled with grain;
they shout for joy and sing.

Psalm 65:11–13

You intended to harm me, but God intended it
for good to accomplish what is now being done,
the saving of many lives.

Genesis 50:20

If I go up to the heavens, you are there;
if I make my bed in the depths, you are there.
If I rise on the wings of the dawn,
if I settle on the far side of the sea,
even there your hand will guide me,
your right hand will hold me fast.

Psalm 139:8–10

How will you use the years God gives you? Will you
be remembered for being a fault finder? Or will you be
known for your quick smile, the laugh lines around your
eyes, and the twinkle deep within? After all, the Lord
gives you your face, but you provide the expression!

Barbara Johnson

A little child was walking one evening with his mother.
He looked up at the sky and said, "Mommy, if the
wrong side of heaven is this beautiful, imagine what the
right side looks like!" Maybe we don't amount to much.
But imagine how we'll look when we're turned right
side out.

Barbara Johnson

Each day, each moment is so pregnant with eternity
that if we "tune in" to it, we can hardly contain the joy. I
have a feeling this is what happened to Moses when he
saw the burning bush. Maybe Yahweh performed laser
surgery on his eyes so he could see what was always
there. And Moses was just so overwhelmed
by the "glory" of God that the very ground he
stood on became infused with "holiness" and
the bushes along the mountain path burned
with splendor.

Gloria Gaither

Several years ago I read a story that often comes to mind when I think about the wisdom of taking life slowly.

It seems that some African missionaries had hired a number of native workers to carry their supplies from one village to another. The missionaries, possessed of the American "push-rush-hurry" mentality, verbally prodded their native employees every day to go a little faster and a little farther than they had the day before. Finally, after three days of being pushed and hurried, the native workers sat down and refused to move.

"What in the world is the problem?" the American missionaries wanted to know. "We have been making excellent time. There's no need to stop here."

"It is not wise to go so rapidly," the spokesman for the native workers explained. "We have moved too fast yesterday. Now today we must stop and wait here for our souls to catch up with our bodies."

Don't you love that? "Wait here for our souls to catch up with our bodies." What a powerful philosophy.

Pausing for a moment here and there takes conscious effort, especially at first, but it will eventually become a habit, and the habit will turn into a way of life. In fact, it will most probably become a foundation stone in one's value system, because we simply cannot live fully or wisely without slowing down, without putting on the brakes, without awareness of each moment.

Luci Swindoll

I continue to love recess. Wheee! I have learned along the journey how important play is to our lives, as long as it is our minor and not our major. We were designed to work and to work heartily. I don't think there is any sweeter sleep than that which follows a diligent day's work. But without respite, work will wear us to a frazzle. Recess keeps the dazzle in our footwork.

Patsy Clairmont

I believe that God is in our everyday, no matter whether we see him, feel him, or hear him. Many moments occur in our lives which reveal his face, his touch, his voice. Look for him today. He will be found. You will be sweetly surprised at the many ways he surrounds you with his love.

Kathy Troccoli

To him who is able to keep you from falling and to present you before his glorious presence without fault and with great joy—to the only God our Savior be glory, majesty, power and authority, through Jesus Christ our Lord, before all ages, now and forevermore! Amen.

Jude vv. 24–25

The LORD has done what he planned;
he has fulfilled his word,
which he decreed long ago.

Lamentations 2:17

The ways of the LORD are right;
the righteous walk in them,
but the rebellious stumble in them.

Hosea 14:9

What about those of us who'd like to turn back the clock? Sure, we'd like to be younger and stronger again. More resilient. But remember Isaiah? He said to let the past lie. Look ahead. Someone has said, "Don't look back. You're not going that way." It is never too late to spend time on the important things. This minute is a gift. That's why we call it the present.

Barbara Johnson

Hugger-mugger looks and sounds like a made-up word, but it's not. It's an in-the-dictionary word that means "confusion; muddle; disordered" — in other words, one of life's tough times. My personal definition is, "I'm so confused I don't know from one minute to the next whether I'll be hugged or mugged." Prayer is the best way to help a friend through a tough time. Even secular research is discovering that prayer works. But of course, we knew it all along.

Sue Buchanan

If you are sick of your mundane life, make a few alterations. Next time you're in the grocery store, buy a package of flower seeds and plant them in a little bed in your backyard just for your soul. Water and tend it every day.

Find a new way to greet the day. Take a different route to work, even if it takes longer. Leave earlier and play your favorite music all the way to the office — sing along at the top of your lungs.

Plan a trip with a good friend and start saving a little money each month. It can be done.

The point is, don't let the beaten path you travel daily beat you down. If you want to see new sights, hear different sounds, speak refreshing words, leave your baggage of fear, regret, guilt, and disappointment behind you and say, "I'm outta here. I'm going to try another way of getting to joy." This new venture may seem scary or strange to you, but don't let that stop you.

Luci Swindoll

Next time you encounter someone in pain, don't just wince and pass by with a shrug. Hurting people need a bit of color to brighten their dark places, and they need to remember the promise that God is with them right where they are. Where rainbows grow, angels sing, and courage becomes contagious. You can be a rainbow gardener by opening your heart even if you're in pain yourself. Let someone know that although you don't have it all together, you find comfort and hope in the Lord.

Barbara Johnson

Are you feeling long on need and short on resources today? Let me encourage you to do what I do when I feel that way: go to the One who has promised to provide everything you need, in abundance. God may not give you the answer you had envisioned, but you can trust it to be the perfect provision. He has promised his fullness. No half remedies. No special deals.

Luci Swindoll

Before anything can be planted, the soil must be ready.
We must allow the softening mulch of God's forgiveness
to give air and breath to the soil of our hearts.
Prejudices—taught in our childhood or imposed by our
society—must be released. Fear must be replaced by
trust, and suspicion by childlike hope and acceptance.
These changes in the soil will not come easily or without
sweat, but any good gardener knows that preparing the
soil is the most important of all labors. It gives the seed
a chance to grow and, eventually, to exhibit all that is
hidden in its complex genetic structure.

Peggy Benson

When we realize our days here matter, our pain has
significance, and our choices are meaningful. We
can step through the darkest of times with hope in
our hearts. It's not that we won't waver, but even our
inquiries have the potential, when we are seeking, to
lead us to a stronger faith. I find that my joy is enlarged
by understanding that, as a child of God, even my pain
has purpose. That realization doesn't eliminate my pain,
but it makes it more manageable, allowing me other
emotions in the midst of calamity, including shocking-
pink joy.

Patsy Clairmont

A thin line separates laughter and pain, comedy and
tragedy, humor and hurt. Our lives constantly walk
that line. When we slip off on one side or the other,
we're taken by surprise. But who said there wouldn't be
surprises? Knowing God just means that all the rules
will be fair; at the end of our life drama, we'll see that.
We never know how things will turn out, but if we know
with certainty they will make sense regardless of how
they turn out, we're onto something.

Barbara Johnson

I want to do. I want to say. I want to act. I'm so guilty of getting in the way of God's timing. To learn to wait has been so difficult for me. I want to "fix" things quickly: the comment someone said about me; the comment I said about someone; the sudden news that turns my whole world upside down; the misunderstanding; the wanting to prove my point or the validity of my character; the uncomfortable changes life often brings.

I would like God to involve himself in my circumstance according to my timing and my agenda. I forget how holy and perfect his ways, his timing, and his agenda are. Yet, over and over I see that when I wait, letting him be God, then he is God.

Kathy Troccoli

If joy were the only emotion God intended us to feel, he could just zap us and take us to heaven right now. Instead, we are left facing a dead end. At such moments, God offers strength so that we won't give in to despair, but be salt in the world, ministering to those around us who are hurting too.

Barbara Johnson

Think about your fears. How many of the feared
disasters never actually came to pass, or if they did,
how many of them really were more than you could
handle? Mark Twain said, "I am an old man and have
known a great many troubles, but most of them never
happened." We waste a great deal of energy dreading
devastation that often never happens.

Sheila Walsh

Have you ever had a dream or a creative idea that you
believed came from God? Since it came from God, he
must be telling you to do it now, right? In your mind
you're thinking, Oh, what a good God! He expects me
to use my intellect, academic competence, position,
status, and accomplishments to take control of this
situation and get what I'm after. I'm a logical, analytical
human being. I know what I'll do, I'll just...

When we surrender our will to the Father, as Jesus
did, we don't need to be concerned about how things
will come out. God has promised the very best for us.
Waiting is hard, I know. But false starts don't get us
anywhere we want to go either.

Thelma Wells

*The LORD is gracious and compassionate,
    slow to anger and rich in love.*

Psalm 145:8

*Satisfy us in the morning with your unfailing love,
    that we may sing for joy and be glad all
    our days.
May the favor of the Lord our God rest upon us;
    establish the work of our hands for us.*

Psalm 90:14, 17

*God is our refuge and strength,
    an ever-present help in trouble.
Therefore we will not fear.*

Psalm 46:1–2

Friendship is a word full of growth potential. One can become bigger (as in character enlargement), or one can become smaller (as in narrow-minded). Becoming a good friend is aerobic in that it takes time and effort. When Jesus is our best friend, we won't approach human friendships from such a shallow place. When we turn to him first and then turn to others, we will be better prepared to give and receive relationally and rationally.

Patsy Clairmont

The giggles in life usually come from little things. If we train ourselves to look for them, see them, and then giggle with them or even at them, we get a "perk." Seeing these potential breaks from routine sometimes requires that we adjust the lenses through which we see life. That adjustment can be as simple as heightening our awareness of the quirky and unusual around us. Giggle potential is everywhere; we just need to slow down long enough to see it.

Marilyn Meberg

Sometimes I think God is smiling while I rant and rave and pound on the floor objecting to the unfairness of life. It's like God is saying, "Come on, Barbara, is that the best you can do? I can take more than that."

God has a better sense of humor than any of us. He may laugh at our tantrums—in a good-natured way. Other times I think he just ignores them, because while we're begging him to change things, he sees the bigger picture.

Barbara Johnson

I sometimes forget that life is fragile. The fact that I have more time to dream my dreams and take my ease is no reason at all to disregard the moment I'm in by preferring to be somewhere else. I have to remind myself that wherever I am—fast lane or slow lane, in traffic or out of traffic, racing or resting—God is there. He is in me, abiding in me, thus making it possible for me to be all there, myself.

Luci Swindoll

I was driving down a familiar road one fall day when I almost drove off the road; the beauty was so intense. It looked as if God had sent in a team of the world's finest artists overnight—and I was privy to the opening day of his spectacle. As I slowly drove along this festive row, leaves danced in the air and brushed against my windshield. It seemed as if I had landed in Oz. I was strongly tempted to get out and clap at God's imagination.

Sheila Walsh

"No eye has seen
   no ear has heard,
no mind has conceived what God has prepared
   for those who love him."

1 Corinthians 2:9

Jesus said, "In this world you will have trouble...
But take heart! I have overcome the world."

John 16:33

Cast all your anxiety on him because he cares
for you.

1 Peter 5:7

The LORD is my light and my salvation —
   whom shall I fear?

Psalm 27:1

I sought the LORD, and he answered me;
   he delivered me from all my fears.

Psalm 34:4

God Always Has a Plan B

Whatever your time, whatever your season, even
in the midst of tragedy, there are moments worth
savoring. Some of us have more sand on the bottom
of our hourglass than at the top. (I'm not referring to
our figures, even though they do tend to slip with the
sand.) Yet, as long as breath is in our bodies, there will
be moments, sweet moments, to revel in. This time is
our time. Let's go savor the flavor!

Patsy Clairmont

My husband used to say, "In this life, if you have two
or three good friends, consider yourself fortunate." My
friends are the part of my life that gives me warmth,
color, texture, courage, comfort, strength, joy, tears,
and, very often, laughter. If I were asked what I cherish
most, my answer would surely be my faith in God, but
without so much as a comma between, I would have to
add my exquisite treasure of friends and family. This is
a collection I intend to keep.

Peggy Benson

If we would just take time with him ... make time for
him. Not just surviving with Jesus, but thriving with
Jesus. Pursuing him as he pursues us. We would be so
much more in tune with what his desires are for us.

Kathy Troccoli

42

Sometimes, despite our best intentions, we find ourselves wandering in a wilderness of anxiety, lost and unable to find our way out. I know. For years I felt that way. Nothing seemed to work; I felt stripped and anxious, unable to determine what my mission in life should be. What was I aiming for? Where was a map out of this hazy land in which I wandered but couldn't find the path out? It wasn't that I hadn't set goals. It's that I didn't know how to set my sights on God and let him lead me.

Thelma Wells

There is no situation in this life that God will not miraculously lead us through — giving us a strength and peace that we know is beyond anything we could conjure up. Lean on him. Abandon yourself to his grace. God will give you strength when you need it.

Kathy Troccoli

God never gives up on us no matter how hard we try to get ourselves loose. God does not let go. That doesn't mean he controls everything we do. It doesn't mean he puts a bridle on us and leads us by the nose. He gives each one of us free will and common sense and a spirit that can communicate with his. When we go through afflictions, he allows us to choose our response. But no matter what our response may be, he sticks around to the bitter end.

Barbara Johnson

Through the maze and amazement of many years of relationships, I have learned that all friends aren't meant to be for a lifetime. In the garden of friendship, too, there are annuals and perennials. Some demand careful tending while others flourish with little attention. It helps to remember that though human relationships, like flowers, require human intervention, a sovereign Master Gardener is in charge. He plans not only the original mix of genus, color, height, fullness, and durability, but he knows exactly in what space and at what time each can bloom to its full potential and complement and nourish (or draw nourishment from) the others. And when the garden's self-sustaining cycle is diminished, he lovingly makes divine provision for rest and regeneration.

Joy MacKenzie

At times I feel as if the events of my life are riding on a pink golf ball that suddenly curves off in a direction I didn't plan, didn't want, and over which I have no control. In dismay, I watch as my life careens off the course I have carefully planned for it. And, as in my rescue of my pink golf ball, I have to wander off my chosen course to reinstitute my life. While this is an adventuresome experience, it is not a selected or joyous one.

I've also experienced many unexpected curves that were delightful and enriching. I didn't see them coming, nor did I have time to prepare; they were just suddenly there.

But life is simply full of curves—sometimes gentle, pleasant, and surprisingly gratifying, and sometimes threatening to overwhelm me in their sharpness. The seat belt insuring my survival is that one profound and simple truth: Jesus loves me.

Marilyn Meberg

Life isn't a destination, but a journey, and so we
all encounter unexpected curves, turning points,
mountaintops, and valleys. We discover the best in
ourselves as each event occurs and shapes us into who
we are. The trip can be a long one, but we can support
each other on the way by loving, caring, and softening
the blows.

God is the one who knows our future and the paths we
will take during our journey. He fine-tunes us and shapes
our foliage so those who are watching can admire his
handiwork in us. And we can be assured that, because of
him, life will always offer us beautiful vistas.

Barbara Johnson

We can reinsert humor and joy into our lives, even
though factors that deplete us of cheer can't be
changed. Some of the "stuff" of life is mundane and
draining, while other parts of life are enormous and
hard. Whatever the size of the difficulty, cheer is
waiting to be discovered—sometimes unexpectedly,
like a chocolate chip in the Raisin Bran.

Marilyn Meberg

Do not lose heart. Though outwardly we are wasting away, yet inwardly we are being renewed day by day. For our light and momentary troubles are achieving for us an eternal glory that far outweighs them all.

2 Corinthians 4:16–17

Jesus said, "All things are possible with God."

Mark 10:27

The joy of the LORD is your strength.

Nehemiah 8:10

More and more, I'm learning to embrace what life has to offer, to soak the poison out of it by taking in God's love in a way that helps me do, act, and say exactly what is in his heart to do, act, and say. And I only become a better person for it. My heart continues to grow wider so that more of Jesus can dwell in me.

Kathy Troccoli

Are you letting the sorrow and the what-ifs of life rob you of the joy of what is? We need to continue on, to drive through the construction with our heats set on seeing what it is that God is doing in us as we drive through the hurt.

Barbara Johnson

Strong friendships almost always involve self-sacrifice. People who don't wish to be inconvenienced or embarrassed or deal with a long, long list of other impositions and annoyances, don't usually endure. Almost every human relationship is messy once in awhile. Being a real friend means giving freely and expecting nothing in return. That's the Christ model!

Peggy Benson

As a child, I pictured the true Christian as being a missionary. Here's what she looked like: Bangs cut extra short so that she wouldn't need another haircut for at least six months. The rest of her hair pulled so tightly in a bun that she looked permanently surprised. (There would be no room for impure thoughts, as they were all strangled to death.) A true Christian? Maybe not! We are made in the image of God, to be loving, faithful, true, compassionate, kind, creative, righteous, strong, tender, eternal.

Sheila Walsh

We need not set out in search for a friend ... rather, we must simply set out to be the friend Christ modeled—anticipating the needs of others, wearing ourselves out at giving. Jesus died doing it. The rewards are infinite and joyous!

Peggy Benson

49

The events of our lives, when we let God use them, become the mysterious and perfect preparation for the work he has called us to. The truth is that our trials are a furnace forging us into gold.

Barbara Johnson

A darling young mother once gave me the idea to tack up these letters where I will see them—TICDAABGC—and make a list underneath: THINGS I CANNOT DO ANYTHING ABOUT BUT GOD CAN. This reminds me there are always things we can't change, but we can get on with our lives and leave those things up to God.

Barbara Johnson

Keep looking to God. Keep trusting in him. Know that he is always leading you to a higher place—let him. The road may look strange to you. You may even feel lost, or far behind, or confused. But if you follow Jesus, it will be the right road; and in the end you will have peace. For peace is found only in the center of God's will.

Kathy Troccoli

I will rejoice in the LORD,
I will be joyful in God my Savior.
The Sovereign LORD is my strength;
he makes my feet like the feet of a deer,
he enables me to go on the heights.

Habakkuk 3:18–19

I know that you can do all things;
no plan of yours can be thwarted.

Job 42:2

Those who plan what is good find love
and faithfulness.

Proverbs 14:22

The LORD watches over the way of the righteous,
but the way of the wicked will perish.

Psalm 1:6

God Always Has a Plan B

Holy moments come to us daily if we will ask for eyes to see. It may be the sun streaming through the window as you fold laundry. Or maybe it's lifting your friends to God while you vacuum. We can't always withdraw to quiet hillsides to pray, but Christ will meet with us in the quiet places of our hearts.

Sheila Walsh

When I look at my calendar, it amazes me that, in the grand scheme of things, I have any friends at all. Of course, there is only one reasonable explanation for the great gift of true friendship, and that lies in the Maker of the Universe who has drawn every minute plan for my life.

Joy MacKenzie

The God of the universe has chosen you to know him! It's like crawling out of a ditch, covered in mud and debris, and being put on the best-dressed list. It's like being handed the Pulitzer Prize for literature when you can barely write your own name. It's like showing up with empty pockets at a benefit dinner for the needy and being voted benefactor of the year.

Sheila Walsh

Sometimes at the end of a busy day, when I think about all the things I never got around to, I try to look at things differently: upside down, inside out, or with light shining on the dark side. It's like the eclipse of the sun: Most people don't pay much attention to the light—or the lighthearted parts of life—until they are covered by darkness. Then, suddenly, lightheartedness becomes dramatic.

Kids love the way light shines through crystal, ricochets off diamonds, emanates from rainbows. Crystals, diamonds, and rainbows are all designed by God. He put them in the world to remind us to take things lightly. He means for us to wonder and imagine what could be hidden in the darkest piece of coal or the rainiest day on earth. Thinking we know it all closes our hearts to what is beautiful and new.

Barbara Johnson

Courage and fear are strange bedmates. It would seem to be impossible to have one and have the other too, and yet I believe that is the challenge of the Christian life. Courage and fear belong together. Fear tells us that life is unpredictable, anything can happen; courage replies quietly, "Yes, but God is in control." As Oswald Chambers said, "When you fear God you fear nothing else, whereas if you do not fear God, you fear everything else."

Sheila Walsh

Remember that the right temperature in a home is maintained by warm hearts, not by icy glares, lukewarm enthusiasm, or hotheads! Your attitude can set the tone for your whole family. So use whatever scraps you can find—even if, in the beginning, it's just a scrap of a smile—and make a gift of whatever you have. Then watch the gifts come back to you.

Barbara Johnson

Your light will break forth like the dawn,
and your healing will quickly appear;...
Then you will find your joy in the LORD,
and I will cause you to ride on the heights
of the land.

Isaiah 58:8, 14

Show me your ways, O LORD,
teach me your paths;
guide me in your truth and teach me,
for you are God my Savior,
and my hope is in you all day long.

Psalm 25:4–5

Trust in the LORD with all your heart
and lean not on your own understanding;
in all your ways acknowledge him,
and he will make your paths straight.

Proverbs 3:5–6

When God said a joyful heart (or laughing heart) is good medicine, I believe he was literal in his meaning. The medical world has verified that laughter releases endorphins, God's natural painkillers, which are fifty to one hundred times more powerful than morphine. Don't you love that? The God of the universe has said all along that a joyful heart is good medicine. God has given us a prescription. All we have to do is fill the prescription.

Marilyn Meberg

Running to hide our faces in God is not like seeking the comfort and familiarity of a childhood blanket that allows us to tune out the realities of our lives. God is a mighty lion, whose roar is heard in every corner of the world. Still, when you are in trouble, you can hide your face from him or run to him and let him hide you in his mane. There you will find strength to live your life.

Sheila Walsh

When from the ashes of bitter disappointment, new dreams rise like a phoenix on the strong wings of a new morning, and when we look back down the long road of our lives and see piles of ash like altars built along our path, we feel a simple chorus rising in our hearts: "Jesus is all that I need." He smiles at us—we know it—and whispers simply: "I am."

Gloria Gaither

You can be a blessing to the people you meet today. Yes, life has its serious moments. But being just a bit kooky may be the secret to seeing yourself and others through good times and bad. Go ahead, make someone's day—make her smile.

Thelma Wells

Some say the best way to forget your troubles is to wear tight shoes, but I say go out and hug somebody.

Barbara Johnson

God Always Has a Plan B

Studies say that people who have friends live longer and have fewer illnesses, and that a close circle of friends actually helps the immune system work. With this in mind, run, don't walk, to your nearest neighborhood coffee klatch, church group, political club, or neighborhood bar. (Just kidding about the bar, but you get the drift!) You won't find that "close circle of friends" by sitting at home reading *National Enquirer* and watching TV! You do want your immune system to work, don't you?

Peggy Benson

Why do I sometimes get bogged down with chores, hating the day? Then, at other items, I get fired up with enthusiasm, loving the day? Perspective! Perspective is everything. Paul encourages us to do whatever we do with all our hearts. He tells us to put our soul into it. Like the old song says, "You gotta have heart." When we do, we can do anything. The busiest days can become our most joyful.

We all have things in life we have to do, but we can choose how we want to do them. It's up to each of us. I can tell you this, though. There's only one way to have joy … by doing everything "as unto the Lord."

Luci Swindoll

He has not left himself without testimony: He has shown kindness by giving you rain from heaven and crops in their seasons; he provides you with plenty of food and fills your hearts with joy.

Acts 14:17

Every good and perfect gift is from above, coming down from the Father of the heavenly lights, who does not change like shifting shadows.

James 1:17

God Always Has a Plan B

Don't take yourself too seriously. It just makes life all the harder. It'll all come out in the wash anyway, because God's glory eventually will eclipse everything that goes wrong on this earth. Lighten up and learn to laugh at yourself. None of us is infallible. We make mistakes in life, and more often than not, they're funny. Sometimes, being your own source of comedy is the most fun of all.

Luci Swindoll

When you live in the present moment, time stands still. Accept your circumstances and live them. If there is an experience ahead of you, have it! But if worries stand in your way, put them off until tomorrow. Give yourself a day off from worry. You deserve it.

Some people live with a low-grade anxiety tugging at their spirit all day long. They go to sleep with it, wake up with it, carry it around at home, in town, to church, and with friends. Here's a remedy: Take the present moment and find something to laugh at. People who laugh, last.

Barbara Johnson

My experience with the prompting of the Holy Spirit has been that when he does, there is an indescribable peace in your body, mind, and spirit that you feel but can't explain to anyone who hasn't experienced it. And, of course, God's Spirit would never direct us to do anything contrary to Scripture, so we have a guidebook that can help us. You've probably said in certain situations, "I knew in my heart that such and such was ..." or, "I had a feeling that ..." Those are probably times God's Spirit is prompting you.

I have found the Holy Spirit to be the greatest organizer, time manager, administrator, arbitrator, and scheduler. What will you do when you think you're being prompted by the Holy Spirit to take a certain action? I'd suggest you ask for clarity. Wait for the answer. I can't tell you how you will know when the answer comes, but I can tell you that you will experience peace in your mind, body, and soul that you can't describe. Listen to your heart.

Thelma Wells

God Always Has a Plan B

The development of a laugh attitude begins internally. It begins with a foundation that is God-inspired and God-constructed. That foundation gives us security as we stand confidently on the strength of his incomparable love for us. Faith in that solid foundation then leads to personal rest and divine security. Without this internal peace, the laughter inspired by all the zany antics we can think of will ultimately die in the wind, leaving a hollow void waiting to be filled with the next antic or joke.

Marilyn Meberg

However humble our circumstances or undramatic our talents, our true purpose has been revealed. We were meant to be this person at this time and place. Not only for ourselves, but also for other people—we were meant to make this particular contribution to the world.

And so we must do it well. Do it with faith and patience, with all our strength and passion. And in so doing discover who we really are.

Marjorie Holmes

Instead of their shame
my people will receive a double portion,
and instead of disgrace
they will rejoice in their inheritance...
and everlasting joy will be theirs.

Isaiah 61:7

Search me, O God, and know my heart;
test me and know my anxious thoughts.
See if there is any offensive way in me,
and lead me in the way everlasting.

Psalm 139:23–24

Cast your cares on the LORD
and he will sustain you;
he will never let the righteous fall.

Psalm 55:22

When I say, "The Lord is my Shepherd, I shall not be in want," it's more than just something to recite before eating. It's an affirmation that the Good Shepherd is watching over all the affairs of my life and is making sure I'm taken care of. The next time you hear this verse, concentrate on the assurance that you can depend on him to watch over you, to protect you, to provide for you, to comfort you, to chastise you when you need it, to bandage your wounds, to calm your fears, to care for your relationships, to communicate with you, and to love you unconditionally. You shall not be in want.

Thelma Wells

Maybe I'm just a cockeyed optimist, but I think life is to be experienced joyfully rather than endured grudgingly. We know it brings complexities and trouble. Scripture affirms that. But why do we take minor irritations so seriously? Why do we act as though it's the end of the world? Think of the pain and the conflict we would spare ourselves, the stress we would forego,
if we just realized mere inconveniences can be survived.

Luci Swindoll

Remember, a small trouble is like a pebble. Hold it too close to your eye, and it puts everything out of focus. Hold it at proper viewing distance, and it can be examined and classified. Throw it at your feet and see it in its true setting—just one more tiny bump on the pathway.

Barbara Johnson

When the hard times of life come, we know that no matter how tragic the circumstances seem, no matter how long the spiritual drought, no matter how long and dark the days, the sun is sure to break through; the dawn will come. The warmth of his assurance will hold us in an embrace once again, and we will know that our God has been there all along. We will hear him say, through it all, "Hold on, my child, joy comes in the morning!"

Gloria Gaither

And we know that in all things God works for the good
of those who love him, who have been called
according to his purpose.

Romans 8:28

The LORD bless you
    and keep you;
the LORD make his face shine upon you
    and be gracious to you;
the LORD turn his face toward you
    and give you peace.

Numbers 6:24–26

The LORD does whatever pleases him.

Psalm 135:6

Can't you tell when you're with someone who's listening? She hears you, really hears you. She hears the sadness in your tone or catches your joy. Be a listener, to music, to life, to others, to God. Life is noisy, but there is music in every heartbeat. God is waiting to bring joy and peace to the confusion of our days.

Sheila Walsh

It's true that goals help us to be disciplined and to aim our energies toward accomplishing what we've set out to do. So goals in and of themselves aren't bad. But for me, setting goals and not leaning on God had led me into a perplexing and fretful place I didn't want to go back to. I had learned that first I needed to humbly go before God and give him my concerns. Then he would provide me with direction. But the relinquishment and sweet repose were what I wanted to concentrate on.

You may be in the same wilderness I was, anxiously wandering around, feeling aimless and without a map, fearful that disaster is headed toward you. Relinquish your anxieties to God. For he cares for you. Directions will come in God's good time—and so will sweet sleep.

Thelma Wells

God Always Has a Plan B

Had I set out to cultivate the perfect group of friends,
I would likely have omitted most of the people who have
become my dearest companions. Fortunately, in God's
sovereign plan, friendships rise naturally—often out of
what we see as unnatural alliances or circumstances.
What a relief to know that he is the one in charge.

Peggy Benson

Sometimes life becomes so complicated we feel as
if we've gone as far as we can down this stressful
highway. We imagine ourselves smashed up against a
brick wall, unable to answer one more call, hear one
more complaint, and take one more breath. When that's
the image that fills your mind, change the brick wall to
God. Imagine yourself pressed tightly against his heart,
wrapped in his everlasting arms, soothed by his life-
giving breath. Picture yourself encircled in God's love,
soaked in his strength.

Barbara Johnson

We can hold on to things and stay in places of
brokenness. We can go on in ways that are false in
healing and false in peace. And, in doing so, we can
suffer the tragedy of missing God's heart. Or we can
lay down our lives in celebration to let God do as he
wishes with us.

Kathy Troccoli

The way of the LORD is a refuge for the righteous.

Proverbs 10:29

The LORD will do what is good in his sight.

2 Samuel 10:12

I will sing to the LORD,
*   for he is highly exalted....*
The LORD is my strength and my song;
*   he has become my salvation....*
In your unfailing love you will lead
*   the people you have redeemed.*
In your strength you will guide them
*   to your holy dwelling.*

Exodus 15:1–2, 13

A man's ways are in full view of the LORD,
*   and he examines all his paths.*

Proverbs 5:21

[Jesus] said to me, "My grace is sufficient for you, for my power is made perfect in weakness." ... That is why, for Christ's sake, I delight in weaknesses, in insults, in hardships, in persecutions, in difficulties. For when I am weak, then I am strong.

2 Corinthians 12:9–10

Shout for joy, O heavens;
  rejoice, O earth;
  burst into song, O mountains!
For the LORD comforts his people
  and will have compassion on his afflicted ones.

Isaiah 49:13

As for God, his way is perfect.

2 Samuel 22:31

In the day of my trouble I will call to you,
  for you will answer me.

Psalm 86:7

The best thing about this very minute is your ability to recognize the possibilities in it. Any fool can count the seeds in an apple. But only God can count the apples in a seed. There is something in every problem that holds potential for something better. Do you want a lifetime of happy right nows? The little choice this moment to see the beauty in what appears ugly, frustrating, or disgraceful will change everything. You have 1,440 minutes in every day. That's 525,600 minutes per year.

Barbara Johnson

Hungry souls are everywhere. Be watchful. Remain open. God will fill your eyes with compassion, your words with wisdom, and your heart with mercy. Introduce the world to love. Introduce the world to Jesus.

Kathy Troccoli

Things aren't always as easy as we would like. But if you keep on keeping on, you can make it. Every road has an end; every mountain has its peak. If we can just hold on and keep climbing, knowing that God is aware of how we're straining, he will bring us over and up the mountains. It's consoling to know God is in control of every part of our journey to glory, even over the steep mountains.

Thelma Wells

As changes take place in my life, I continue to watch them truly work out for my good—if I can just wait on God to see me through. What makes all the difference is trust—the understanding that God has a much bigger plan than mine even if I don't understand it. I'm grateful, yet sorry, that I have had to learn so many lessons by hindsight.

Kathy Troccoli

Rejoice in the Lord always. I will say it again: Rejoice! Let your gentleness be evident to all. The Lord is near. Do not be anxious about anything, but in everything, by prayer and petition, with thanksgiving, present your requests to God. And the peace of God, which transcends all understanding, will guard your hearts and your minds in Christ Jesus.

Philippians 4:4–7

I lift up my eyes to the hills—
*   where does my help come from?*
My help comes from the LORD,
*   the Maker of heaven and earth.*

Psalm 121:1–2

God Always Has a Plan B

You and I know about the worst and grossest and most detestable things that can possibly happen. But we serve a God who is a Master. He can transform the blackest black to the purest white. As I hear the stories of thousands of people all over this country, I am amazed at the very different ways God brings good out of what Satan meant for bad. There is no doubt in my mind that if you do not see it in the present moment, it is in process. It's like they say about the weather in England: if you don't like it, wait a minute. There is nothing outside the reach of God. With time and faith, you'll see the majestic head and loving face of Jesus Christ, the Savior, emerge from your life's worst stain.

Barbara Johnson

Trial and triumph are what God uses to scribble all over the pages of our lives.

Barbara Johnson

At this point in my life the most difficult task that I attempt in any given day is to get clothes on my son. He wriggles. He moves at the wrong moment. Every now and then he'll lie back and bless his mother with the opportunity to clothe him without requiring oxygen at the end of it, and I count my blessings. So, too, we are called to relax in God and allow him to clothe us in his righteousness.

Sheila Walsh

Lily Tomlin says, "For fast-acting relief, try slowing down." Simply put, take a few minutes daily to ponder what is worthwhile about living. Stop whirling about like a pinwheel long enough to come to a rest and consider your next action. Just what is it you want to do? What do you need to do for the sake of your soul?

Luci Swindoll

An English fisherman went into an inn at the end of a long, cold day and ordered a pot of tea. Bragging to friends about his big catch of fish, he stretched out his arm with a sweeping motion. In an instant he knocked the teapot off the table and against the wall. A dark stain splashed across the wallpaper.

The fisherman was aghast at what he had done and apologized profusely to the innkeeper. He tried to wipe off the tea, but already it had made an ugly blotch. Shortly, a man seated at the next table came up and said, "Calm yourself, Sir." The stranger took out a coal pencil and began to sketch around the shape of the stain. In moments he created a picture of a majestic stag that looked as if it had been designed for that wall. Soon he was recognized as Sir Edmond Lancier, England's foremost painter of wildlife.

What Sir Edmond Lancier did with an unsightly tea stain in a fine English inn, our God is doing every day. He is working in the lives of people who wonder how they'll ever recover from the ugly things that have happened to them. He is making masterpieces of our lives that stand as testimonies to his love and power.

Barbara Johnson

The ransomed of the LORD will return.
They will enter Zion with singing;
everlasting joy will crown their heads.
Gladness and joy will overtake them,
and sorrow and sighing will flee away.

Isaiah 35:10

Let the morning bring me word of your
unfailing love,
for I have put my trust in you.
Show me the way I should go,
for to you I lift up my soul.

Psalm 143:8

Be still, and know that I am God.

Psalm 46:10

God Always Has a Plan B

Occasionally I must remind myself that all gifts are given to me, God's beloved child, with incomparable love and joy. For me to feel guilty about buying myself something is to forget the original Author of that gift. And if I forget that reality, I may then lose sight of his all-encompassing love for me. Everything good and loving in life has its source in God, including all gifts.

Marilyn Meberg

Life is a refining process. Our response to it determines whether we'll be ground down or polished up. On a piano, one person sits down and plays sonatas, while another merely bangs away at "Chopsticks." The piano is not responsible. It's how you touch the keys that makes the difference. It's how you play what life gives you that determines your joy and shine.

Barbara Johnson

God doesn't expect us to perform for him. He loves us always—when we're disappointed or hurt or making a mess of things. Sometimes we speak to him in a language that only he can understand. What matters to him is that we are vulnerable, that we are completely ourselves. We are work, too, but God cherishes us.

Luci Swindoll

I drove on, thinking about my current frenzy to get things done—a woman on the go but still God's child. A sense of safety, of well-being, of security came over me, and I wrapped my hand around God's finger. He always has my best interest at heart. He knows exactly where I am. He notices everything.

Kathy Troccoli

God Always Has a Plan B

Sometimes I think my life is like my linen closet—constantly in need of cleaning, discarding, rearranging, and straightening. Unfortunately, linen closets never straighten or clean themselves. Likewise, we can't—by our own power—change our lives. When we open the door and allow God's life-changing power to enter in … step by step, moment by moment … he begins a good work in us. Dead wood is cut out. Discipline is applied. Priorities rearranged. In some areas he works quickly. In others, painfully slow. But his timing is perfect.

Diane Head

We can take distasteful things and turn them into something true and beautiful. That's what God does! He knows change can make your life richer. If you find your current change distressful, encrust it with sequins and feathers, wrap it in gold foil paper, receive it as a gift with delight and appreciation. Live for today but hold your hands open to tomorrow. Anticipate the future and its changes with joy. There is a seed of God's love in every event, every circumstance, every unpleasant situation in which you may find yourself. Don't get stuck in a rut or hung up on an outdated blessing. You serve a God of change!

Barbara Johnson

It's consoling to know God not only doesn't sleep but also doesn't even get drowsy. We can depend on him to attend to our every need twenty-four hours a day, seven days a week. That gives us peace. It's a bitter pill to think that we let others down. We disappoint loved ones. We inconvenience people we care about. But how wonderful, how beautiful, how comforting to know we have a God who is always near to console and cheer, just when we need him most.

Thelma Wells

Perhaps you've heard the expression, "You never have a second chance to make a first impression." It's true; the first impression is usually the lasting impression. But, thanks be to God, sometimes we get another chance. When I create a wrong first impression, I'm consoled to realize God knows us inside out and outside in. He never has to wonder who we are or what we're up to. And if we behave badly sometimes, he understands what motivates us and accepts us even in our worst moments. I want to be able to do the same for others.

Thelma Wells

God invites us to express our uniqueness and have fun by making things with our hands. These things don't have to be big or elaborate or even "correct," but making them should provide solace and personal fulfillment. Handmade things should reflect us: a fine meal, a garden patch, a beautiful quilt, a backdrop for a play, a piece of music, a poem, a letter. The idea is to keep our hands busy with meaningful activity so that we develop inside ourselves, depending upon the Lord and not on others for endorsement or approbation. May God help us to express and define ourselves in our one-of-a-kind way.

Luci Swindoll

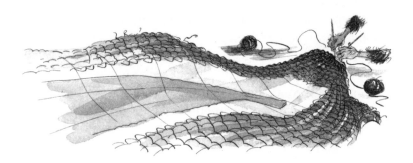

God is amazing. While we may not understand the reasons for everything we must endure in this life, letting him be God is the safest, best, and most comforting place to be. He sees our tears, he wipes them dry, and he delivers everything in his power to meet our greatest needs. He is trustworthy.

Kathy Troccoli

Watch out! God is making you authentic. Real. Rubbing off your fake fur. Changing your outlook. Giving you new desires. Making you marvelous. Fulfilling what you were created for. He is making you the "Queen of Quite a Lot," enlightening you for kingdom work. Open your arms wide to God's imaginative work in you. Be brave. Then braver still. Never resist his insistence on your perfection.

Barbara Johnson

Then maidens will dance and be glad,
    young men and old as well.
I will turn their mourning into gladness;
    I will give them comfort and joy instead
    of sorrow.

Jeremiah 31:13

Then my enemies will turn back
    when I call for help.
    By this I will know that God is for me.

Psalm 56:9

Come near to God and he will come near to you.

James 4:8

God Always Has a Plan B

How will the Lord use your life this year? This month? This day? Is there one thing you can do to make life better for someone else? Can you warm the home of an elderly friend? Chill out so a teenager can open up to your love? Knock on the door of a lonely single mom? Invite a seven-year-old for lemonade? The possibilities are endless. God expects us to use our brains and figure out what we can do to make a difference. Find out where he's working and join his crew.

Barbara Johnson

We all face dangers and heartaches in life because we live in a lost and fallen world. But in the midst of these difficulties, we can be absolutely confident that we are not left alone to deal with them. God's faithfulness is our constant shield. We are covered by the shadow of the Almighty! Oh, the security that is ours in God's promise that he will be with us in trouble!

Hope MacDonald

It's easy to lose sight of the joy that a simple approach to others can bring. But if we close our eyes and wish really hard, we just might recall a tinge of what it's like to experience life as a child.

Barbara Johnson

The circumstances of life can embitter any of us at any time. But if we allow it, God's grace and love can empower us and help us move through these times victoriously.

Kathy Troccoli

Time mellows people as it mellows wine, as long as the grapes are good. You may set out to be a businesswoman, but in the course of time end up caring for a dying parent, orphaned niece, or disabled brother. You may encounter illness yourself, and end up being a writer, touching the heartstrings—not the purse strings—of other people. That's why it's best to always be true to yourself and God and to be flexible within his will. He will use you.

Barbara Johnson

A friend of mine claims we need bumpers—angel bumpers—on our cars to protect us from serious damage. My friend also suggests we equip ourselves with the shock absorber of laughter to make the journey easier and the windshield wipers of God's love to swish away the what-ifs so we can more clearly see what is.

Barbara Johnson

"The fool says in his heart, 'There is no God'" (Psalm 14:1). This designation goes for those who doubt God's sovereignty as well as those who deny him. Either he is sovereign, or he is not God. Therefore, when we become so preoccupied with and dismayed by circumstances and certain people that we doubt God's ability to handle things in his own way, and in his own time, then we, too, are fools.

Ruth Bell Graham

The LORD watches over all who love him.

Psalm 145:20

Because of his great love for us, God, who is rich in mercy, made us alive with Christ even when we were dead in transgressions — it is by grace you have been saved. And God raised us up with Christ and seated us with him in the heavenly realms in Christ Jesus, in order that in the coming ages he might show the incomparable riches of his grace, expressed in his kindness to us in Christ Jesus.

Ephesians 2:4–7

A laugh lifestyle is predicated upon our attitude toward the daily stuff of life. When those tasks seem too dull to endure, figure out a way to make them fun; get creative and entertain yourself. If the stuff of life for you right now is not dull and boring but instead painful and overwhelming, find something in the midst of the pain that makes you smile or giggle anyway. There's always something somewhere … even if you have to just pretend to laugh until you really do!

Marilyn Meberg

How do you change the habits of a lifetime? I love the line of Mark Twain: "You can't break a bad habit by throwing it out the window. You've got to walk it slowly down the stairs." Slowly and deliberately. Walking takes commitment. It takes the first step and the next and the next until you get to the door.

Sheila Walsh

Laughter is the key to surviving the special stresses of the child-rearing years. I believe if you can see the delightful side of your assignment, you can also deal with the difficult. Laughter helps, regardless of your situation. Look for ways to enjoy your day, however small or trivial. Even finding a convenient parking space can bring you joy. Look for fun. Just sitting on a bench and watching people gives us joy in a childlike way.

Barbara Johnson

Shout for joy to the LORD, all the earth.
  Worship the Lord with gladness;
  come before him with joyful songs.
Enter his gates with thanksgiving
  and his courts with praise;
  give thanks to him and praise his name.
For the LORD is good and his love endures forever;
  his faithfulness continues through
    all generations.

Psalm 100:1–2, 4–5

Commit your way to the LORD;
  trust in him.

Psalm 37:5

Whether you turn to the right or to the left,
your ears will hear a voice behind you, saying,
"This is the way; walk in it."

Isaiah 30:21

God Always Has a Plan B

In moments that appear unredeemable, watch and wait. Recognize the precious things. Refuse to trash anything! Ask God to help you see things from His perspective. Take one step after another. Before long, in spite of yourself, you may notice surprising signs of hope in your own backyard: the chuckle of a baby, the kindly light in a neighbor's eyes, the sweet kiss of a spouse, an undreamed of opportunity.

Barbara Johnson

I don't know how God makes things all right; I just know that ultimately he does. Sometimes he reaches out a finger from heaven and in a moment the most hopeless situation is infused with light and life. Sometimes it's as if God closes the book and there is nothing more to say. I don't always understand everything with my mind, but in my spirit I know without a shadow of doubt that God is here. God is still on the throne; it's going to be all right!

Sheila Walsh

Why is it that we limit God? He generally isn't the one who puts the skids on our hopes and dreams. We do it ourselves. We think, "I'm too old," or "I'm not good enough," or "What will people think?" Or "I've never done this before," or "I can't afford it." So we don't even move off home plate. We simply strike out at bat.

The truth is we can't accomplish what is set before us … in and of ourselves. It's best to admit that as soon as possible and then turn our thoughts to this: God is all powerful, and he can do anything. I've tried to crank out so many things in my own strength, never inviting God into the project, and it's absolute work—stressful, tiring—even boring. But every time I turn loose my control and trust God at a deeper level, I learn just a bit more about what God wants to do for me.

Luci Swindoll

Next time you think you hear nothing in response to your prayers, don't assume God isn't listening. He may simply want you to rest in his shadow until he reveals his answer. When you hear a direct no, remind yourself there will always be a better yes. God is for you, and he will work out everything in conformity with the purpose of his will. Everything.

Kathy Troccoli

Each of us has something broken in our lives: a broken promise, a broken dream, a broken marriage, a broken heart ... and we must decide how we're going to deal with our brokenness. We can wallow in self-pity or regret, accomplishing nothing and having no fun or joy in our circumstances; or we can determine with our will to take a few risks, get out of our comfort zone, and see what God will do to bring unexpected delight in our time of need.

Luci Swindoll

I have learned the secret of being content in any and every situation, whether well fed or hungry, whether living in plenty or in want. I can do everything through him who gives me strength.

Philippians 4:12–13

As for God, his way is perfect;
the word of the LORD is flawless.

Psalm 18:30

He guards the course of the just
and protects the way of his faithful ones.

Proverbs 2:8

God Always Has a Plan B

One of my favorite early spring flowers is the Johnny jump-up. They have sweet smiling faces, each with its own personality. They remind me that I have some wonderful jump-up friends in my life—people who have come into my life over the years at just the exact time I needed to see a friendly, smiling face.

Peggy Benson

You never know how God is working through your prayers or how he is using what you try to do, even when you don't see results. Live parenthood to the hilt. Bequeath your kisses and your discipline generously. Raise the standard of faith along with a finger to scold or correct. Spread your arms wide to a kid with a skinned knee. Lift a chin, hold a hand, tickle a foot. Keep the good times glowing. Make sure praise is flowing. You are a parent. Be glad!

Barbara Johnson

God is the One who enables us to savor the moment and grow older joyfully. He provides camaraderie and intimacy through friends and families. No reunion is possible without his arrangement, timing, and protection. He infiltrates the workplace, making it an enjoyable part of living rather than a task to get through hurriedly so we can move on to better things. Our accomplishments are enhanced by knowing we have his approval and are made possible only because he gave us the dream in the first place. It is he who intensifies imagination, beauty, and knowledge. And every day, in our vast country, we see and experience his handiwork in blessings, provisions, and grace. A relationship with him enlarges life.

Marilyn Meberg

Celebrating each new day helps us develop the ability to be grateful for all new moments and for the God who is in each one. The discipline of celebrating each new day influences our attitude toward all of life.

Karen Burton Mains

God Always Has a Plan B

If it takes climbing windmills, marching in a parade, or ascending the down escalator to break out of your little, proper, plastic, grown-up mold, do it. Become a really dingy person, not din-gee but ding-ee. Even if people think you are fresh out of the rubber room.

Barbara Johnson

God's timing does not always coincide with our immediate plans. Sometimes his timing requires that we wait and hope.

Beverly LaHaye

We cannot always head off disaster. Sometimes we discover that the light at the end of the tunnel really is the headlight of an oncoming train. Even so, Satan will not get the victory. Christians will keep on risking their hearts whatever happens.

Barbara Johnson

If you're not happy with who you are, you'll spend precious energy trying to be somebody you're not, and it will wear you out. Think for a moment. Is there anybody in your life you're comparing yourself to? A beautiful sister? An accomplished brother? A friend who never seems to have problems? Well, may I say with all the love in the world: Quit it. That business of comparing is going to make you sick and unproductive, if it hasn't already. You are you. God made you, you. And you are exactly who he wants you to be. Don't be somebody's clone. That person you're trying to be may very well be trying to be you.

Luci Swindoll

Jesus said, "Therefore I tell you, do not worry about your life, what you will eat or drink; or about your body, what you will wear. Is not life more important than food, and the body more important than clothes? Look at the birds of the air; they do not sow or reap or store away in barns, and yet your heavenly Father feeds them. Are you not much more valuable then they? Who of you by worrying can add a single hour to his life?

"And why do you worry about clothes? See how the lilies of the field grow. They do not labor or spin. Yet I tell you that not even Solomon in all his splendor was dressed like one of these. If that is how God clothes the grass of the field, which is here today and tomorrow is thrown into the fire, will he not much more clothe you, O you of little faith? So do not worry, saying, "What shall we eat?" or "What shall we drink?" or "What shall we wear?" For the pagans run after all these things, and your heavenly Father knows that you need them. But seek first his kingdom and his righteousness, and all these things will be given to you as well. Therefore do not worry about tomorrow, for tomorrow will worry about itself. Each day has enough trouble of its own."

Matthew 6:25–34

Whatever your troubles, try looking at them by the light of another source or a different star. Go ahead; don't be afraid. Find a wacky angel, a new twist.... Offer trouble a little serious thought, then turn it upside down and look at it through God-colored glasses. Chew on trouble's possibilities for making you smarter, better, stronger, kinder.

Barbara Johnson

The voice of God is always speaking to us, and always trying to get our attention. But his voice is a "still, small voice," and we must at least slow down in order to listen.

Eugenia Price

I love the sea. I love the certainty and the uncertainty of it, its amazing power and its sweet gentleness. It reminds me that a God who can be explained by the mind is no God at all, but an idol constructed by my own hands or, worse, a house pet on a leash. I must stand beside the ocean often so that I will not forget that. I must never create God in my image. His ways are immeasurably higher than my ways.

Gloria Gaither

God Always Has a Plan B

As the melody of our lives unfolds on a daily basis,
the high point lies in the fact that God is never going
to make a mistake with the motif that he's specifically
designed for us. Whatever he does will endure forever.
He brings out the beauty of harmony and richness as
he directs every facet of our lives. This fact guarantees
that all crises already have been met and overcome
in him. As we live, work, and bear our burdens, be
assured that the melody of our lives is controlled by
the eternal God of the universe who knows us from
beginning to end.

Luci Swindoll

Think about it—we are here for such a short time,
yet what we do here is for eternity. Heaven is our final
home, and while we can't take gold bullion or anything
else with us, we can send some things on ahead. The
love we lavish on those in need will yield results that
last forever. So let's marinate folks in love.

Barbara Johnson

Jesus said, "As the Father has loved me, so have I loved you. Now remain in my love. If you obey my commands, you will remain in my love.... I have told you this so that my joy may be in you and that your joy may be complete."

John 15:9–11

It is God who arms me with strength and makes my way perfect.

2 Samuel 22:33

I will instruct you and teach you in the way you should go; I will counsel you and watch over you.

Psalm 32:8

I fling joy—beyond my next-door neighbor's fence, clear across town, and into the universe. Then it curves right back to me. Sometimes with a whack on the head when I need it. Sometimes with a thwack into my heart. Sometimes landing with a crack at my feet. But it always comes back. No doubt about it.

Barbara Johnson

The key to contentment is to consider. Consider who you are and be satisfied with that. Consider what you have and be satisfied with that. Consider what God's doing and be satisfied with that. You will be amazed at how much more comfortable you'll feel with yourself. Finally, consider this: If contentment cannot be found within yourself, you'll never find it.

Luci Swindoll

I have learned that it isn't necessary to resolve all differences for two people to be friends. I have learned that the space and air between two people are as important to a relationship as the times of unity and closeness. Life is a process and, to God, process is not a means to a goal. Process is the goal of life that keeps us moving closer, always closer to an intimate friendship with him.

Gloria Gaither

You are God's kingdom star. You may be overweight, sport age spots, find a new wrinkle in your face now and then. None of that matters. For your beauty is generated from the inside. Stars don't merely reflect the light of the sun like the moon does. Stars are little suns; they generate their own light.

Barbara Johnson

Praise be to the God and Father of our Lord Jesus Christ! In his great mercy he has given us new birth into a living hope through the resurrection of Jesus Christ from the dead, and into an inheritance that can never perish, spoil or fade—kept in heaven for you.

1 Peter 1:3–4

In God I trust; I will not be afraid.

Psalm 56:11

You guide me with your counsel,
*   and afterward you will take me into glory.*

Psalm 73:24

Someone once said that life is made up of the tender teens, the teachable twenties, the tireless thirties, the fiery forties, the fretful fifties, the serious sixties, the sacred seventies, the aching eighties … shortening breath, death, sod, God. That is our journey, and a happy ending awaits us after we make our way through all the tough stuff.

Barbara Johnson

Looking for the essence of beauty is comprehending and appreciating that quality in an object which is fairer and better than only what our eyes see or our ears hear—whether that be a patch of blue in an overcast sky, the fleeting laughter from a voice we love, or something as unexpected as the rainbow colors in a spot of oil on the driveway.

Luci Swindoll

If you have been going through a difficult period in your life, if you have been crushed by some unkind deed, or if you have lost a loved one and are feeling the pangs of loneliness, remember: The psalmist said that "the Lord is close to the brokenhearted" (Psalms 34:18). Why not take refuge in him?

Wanda K. Jones

Live every day to fulfill your personal mission. God has a reason for whatever season you are living through right now. A season of loss or blessing? A season of activity or hibernation? A season of growth or incubation? You may think you're on a detour, but God knows the best way for you to reach your destination.

Barbara Johnson

At first, we seem to be in control of our lives. We determine to create our own healthy environment. We decide never again to be the victim of other people's choices. But before we know it, life is getting complicated. We realize that we've made some choices we regret, taken some turns we never thought we'd take. Oh, we try to fix it on our own, to cover what our heart is telling us, but if the truth were known, we get up in the morning with a hole in our souls. And in our rare honest moments we know we're no closer to our hopes and dreams than we were at the start.

Perhaps the best thing that can happen to us is to realize that we are not self-sufficient. Like a child, we can take the mess we've made of things to a heavenly Father and say, "O Lord, I wanted so to make something beautiful of my life, but just look." The amazing thing about Jesus is that he doesn't just patch up our lives. He doesn't just "make do" out of what we have left. He gives us a brand-new sheet, a clean slate to start over, all new. He makes us new creations.

Gloria Gaither

The people walking in darkness
    have seen a great light;
on those living in the land of the shadow of death
    a light has dawned.
You have enlarged the nation
    and increased their joy.

Isaiah 9:2–3

The LORD is good to all;
    he has compassion on all he has made.

Psalm 145:9

This is what the LORD says —
"I have summoned you by name; you are mine."

Isaiah 43:1

I will lie down and sleep in peace,
    for you alone, O LORD,
    make me dwell in safety.

Psalm 4:8

In pursuit of a relationship with Jesus, we are being changed into his likeness. At that point, all the bewildering questions may remain unanswered. But—as the old-timers used to say—we are finding we don't have such a gnawing need to know the answers when we know the Answer. We are coming, as the poet Rilke said, to love the question and get more comfortable with the paradox of God. When we trust the author, we don't have to know the story. We just know it will be true.

Gloria Gaither

Our capacity to feel, to think, and to experience is so great—to taste the sweetness of joy that life can bring, to bask in the peace of God, to worship on the mountaintops, to ride high on loving and being loved. All of these are wonderful and precious gifts, and I'm so thankful for them as I journey through this earthly life.

Kathy Troccoli

God Always Has a Plan B

Life boasts very few things that are absolutely dependable, but change is one of them, and it is the one we seem to fear most.

The moon and the ocean both provide exquisite models of the rhythm of life—consistent in their waxing and waning, advance and retreat, ebb and flow. But in our brief earth journey, most of us just haven't quite been able to get the hang of it. We dread the ebbing, fearing the flow will never return. We want it to be all flow.... We demand permanency as a security against loss when, in reality, the only way to keep what we have is to allow it freedom to change and grow....

In God's infinite understanding of the human condition, He reaches out to assuage the dread and fear of change: "Trust me," he says, "I will never leave thee nor forsake thee."

Joy MacKenzie

Every day now I take joy—by refusing to be normal, by refusing to accept the lie that I have to feel miserable about the baggage, the stuff, the sickness, that trails me no matter how I try to hide or outwit it. I choose to do zany, kooky, and funny things to make myself and others laugh.

Barbara Johnson

*Now to him who is able to do immeasurably
more than all we ask or imagine, according
to his power that is at work within us, to him
be glory in the church and in Christ Jesus
throughout all generations, for ever and ever!
Amen.*

Ephesians 3:20–21

*Are not five sparrows sold for two pennies?
Yet not one of them is forgotten by God.
Indeed, the very hairs of your head are all
numbered. Don't be afraid; you are worth
more than many sparrows.*

Luke 12:6–7

*Walk in all the way that the LORD your God has
commanded you, so that you may live
and prosper.*

Deuteronomy 5:33

God Always Has a Plan B

My darling daughter-in-love, Shannon, says life is like a dot-to-dot picture. When you begin, you have no idea what your life is going to turn out to be, she says. You start at one dot, and then another dot appears, and you jump off the first dot to land on the next one, hoping for the best. Sometimes a dot can be a huge, black hole. Occasionally, dots are tear-shaped. On others you feel like dancing—maybe those are the polka dots!

Barbara Johnson

Life is too short to spend it being angry, bored, or dull. That was never God's intention. Maybe boredom and dullness aren't on any list of sins in the Bible, but they will sap your joy if you tolerate them. Fight back by developing and relishing a divine sense of humor, the gift God builds into your personality.

Barbara Johnson

The freeway is the last place we think of slowing down or savoring our present moment. We simply want to get the driving over with, so we tear along with all our gripes and derring-do and madness, sometimes risking our very lives. Whether you're battling traffic with danger and risks on all sides, or sitting in your rocking chair knitting a sweater for your granddaughter, remember to be all there. Wherever you are now is God's provision, not his punishment.

Luci Swindoll

Someone once said, "I used to take each day as it came, one at a time. Now I'm down to a half day at a time!" Growing older is sometimes like climbing a steep hill. You can complain, "Too many rocks in the way and bumps on the road!" Or you can look at it this way, "I'd like to live my life in the fast lane, but I'm married to a speed bump." But the most productive way is to put your intellect and spirit to work doing what you do best.

Barbara Johnson

When I bought some new makeup recently, the salesgirl told me that if I dropped a little BB in the bottle and shook it before each use, the makeup wouldn't get thick and gooey. A day or so later, my husband Bill came in smiling broadly and gave me a huge plastic carton. Inside were 10,000 — that's ten thousand! — BBs. God has given us a good measure, pressed down, shaken together, and running over. But most of the time, we need only one BB.

Barbara Johnson

I think of God as a pretty efficient guy, but he doesn't always operate in the fast lane. He operates quite slowly, in fact, when he needs to. Sometimes he has to, not because of his style, but because of mine. My reluctance, my resistance, my disobedience frequently get in the way of my progress and growth. My reluctance to be still and know that he is God; my resistance to hearing his voice when I don't like what he is saying; my disobedience in pretending I didn't hear him in the first place. He has to wait for me all the time ... not to accomplish the tasks in my life but to accommodate his Spirit in my soul.

Marilyn Meberg

"For I know the plans I have for you," declares the LORD, *"plans to prosper you and not to harm you, plans to give you hope and a future. Then you will call upon me and come and pray to me, and I will listen to you. You will seek me and find me when you seek me with all your heart."*

Jeremiah 29:11–13

The LORD searches every heart and understands every motive behind the thoughts.

1 Chronicles 28:9

There is no wisdom, no insight, no plan that can succeed against the LORD.

Proverbs 21:30

God Always Has a Plan B

Did you know researchers say that the simple act of turning your lips up (instead of down) stimulates good feelings? No matter how down you feel, how rotten, try smiling at yourself in every mirror you pass. First thing in the morning. Last thing at night. Broaden those luscious lips. Twist them toward heaven. You'll feel perkier faster if you smile than you would if you wallowed in gloomy thoughts.

Barbara Johnson

God gives me credit for being able to take more than I think I can take. He wants me to take comfort in the fact that he is close. He isn't going anywhere, and no matter how scary things get, he won't come unglued. Our afflictions are designed not to break us but to bend us toward the eternal and the holy. God sticks with us through it all. One lady who wrote to me summed it up this way: "My heart is wallpapered to God's heart."

Barbara Johnson

The time to be happy is now. The thing to treasure
is exactly what you hold in your hands. No matter
how you try to manipulate reality—forcing changes,
denying what's true, worrying about tomorrow—it is
only by accepting life as it is today that you will become
truly rich. Be happy through everything because today
is the only thing you can be sure of. Right here, right
now, cherish the moment you hold in your hands.

Barbara Johnson

My prayer is that you and I will grow richer and deeper
in our faith so that nothing in this life will cause us to
despair. Our God sees beyond our circumstances and
feelings to his truth, to what really does exist. Trust him.

Kathy Troccoli

We come to God with nothing and we are given
everything. There is nothing you can do to earn it, to
be worthy of this love. It is a gift.

Sheila Walsh

Find rest, O my soul, in God alone;
my hope comes from him.

Psalm 62:5

Though you have not seen [Jesus], you love
him; and even though you do not see him
now, you believe in him and are filled with
an inexpressible and glorious joy, for you are
receiving the goal of your faith, the salvation of
your souls.

1 Peter 1:8–9

Do not be afraid or terrified . . . , for the LORD
your God goes with you; he will never leave you
nor forsake you.

Deuteronomy 31:6

Teach me your way, O LORD,
and I will walk in your truth.

Psalm 86:11

Gardening burns calories, lowers risk of heart attack, slows soil erosion, and provides shelter for a host of micro-life. So hooray for gardening! Get your gloves muddy, your face tanned, and your knees crinkled here on earth. Nurture faith and love. Keep believing in the harvest. God will make something beautiful out of your effort and energy. The most beautiful gardens bloom in the heart!

Barbara Johnson

We cannot protect ourselves from trouble, but we can dance through the puddles of life with a rainbow smile, twirling the only umbrella we need—the umbrella of God's love. His covering of grace is sufficient for any problem we may have.

Barbara Johnson

God Always Has a Plan B

Sometimes the very desire for action leads to the neglect of action. We're so busy searching for the perfect opportunity, the most effective method, the favorable moment—so intent are we on improving on God's timing—that we not only disqualify ourselves for the mission and miss the joy, but an urgent need is left unanswered—forever.

I have often experienced the pull of an inner voice, urging me to call a friend who is in need.... Born of genuine concern for my friend, my determination to provide the most propitious response thwarts the entire effort.

Joy MacKenzie

I have consciously sought after those things which make for value, order, richness, spirit, and wonder, even though I am often unable to verbalize what I feel when I perceive something beautiful. Sometimes it's a pang or a sensation; at other times it is an awareness of joy and security or pure pleasure. In any event, it is a moment to be celebrated. Beauty justifies itself. The fact that it is beyond definition means nothing.

Luci Swindoll

In my home, the hearth is burning with enthusiasm and the light of God. Ruth Graham, wife of the evangelist, Billy, named one of her books *Come Sit by My Laughing Fire*. When I saw that title, I thought, yes, that's it! The laughing fire is one that sputters with joy while it burns away the troubles of the day. God wants you to build a laughing fire on the hearth of your home. Use the fuel of his love to turn trouble into heat and energy for yourself and other people. Stoke the smoldering embers of your passion for life. As the smoke curls from the chimney, other people will be drawn to the sweet aroma of compassion.

Barbara Johnson

Like people, plants are born with personality. The difference is that in his plan for people, God added humor! We nurture and are nourished by our friends in different ways. In his plan for friends, God often paints way outside the lines. The color may not rival that of the flower garden, but the comedy is superb!

Joy MacKenzie

God Always Has a Plan B

In being moms and wives and friends, our most pleasing performances of life, we recognize that we are really a small piece of God's big puzzle. It takes each of us working together, worshiping together, giving everything we have. The crowning achievement is when we see it all come together.

Barbara Johnson

It's time all of us learned a bit more about how to retreat—and be alone with God. What is retreat? It's taking time away from our normal routine. It's making a date with God that nothing will be allowed to intrude on. It can be as simple as setting aside an afternoon to go to the park with a journal, your Bible, a favorite devotional book. Or just sitting under a tree and enjoying the presence of God.

Sheila Walsh

People need each other—no matter how much we insist we don't. Nobody is an island, an entity unto herself, or a Lone Ranger. We're in this thing called community, and part of the joy of community is sharing the weight. The weight of burdens, losses, loneliness, and defeat. Look around you, my friend. Who's there for you? And who are you there for? Take a careful look. Even those who insist they can make it on their own may just be waiting for you to reach out and help. Be there and available.

Luci Swindoll

Over the years, God has been faithful to his work, protecting me and providing for me at every turn. I've never regretted my decision to trust God.

My experience underscores the importance of those few profound moments in each person's life, where a significant choice is to be made. Moments when the choice to walk with God, or to go our own way, will have consequences for the rest of our lives. It is at such times that our compassionate Father draws closest, whispering love and hope in our hearts.

Ritz Schweitz

God Always Has a Plan B

When we bring sunshine into the lives of others, we're warmed by it ourselves. When we spill a little happiness, it splashes on us. Hope uncovers new possibilities and shows us what can be done. It wrestles with angels, looks impossibilities in the eye and winks. Hope springs eternal. Hope supersedes all good intentions. Keep going by the power of God's grace. Dare to believe that he has planned greater things right around the corner.

Barbara Johnson

God's Word gives hope when we feel utterly alone and hopeless. We can take comfort in knowing that God does not allow a trial in our lives that is too great for us to bear. We can also be assured that death does not conquer those who die in Christ. God is in charge of all things.

Carol L. Baldwin

Don't be afraid of mistakes or defeats; they are building blocks for all your successes. Remember, determination and faithfulness are the nails used to build the house of God's dreams.

Barbara Johnson

Do not conform any longer to the pattern of this world, but be transformed by the renewing of your mind. Then you will be able to test and approve what God's will is — his good, pleasing and perfect will.

Romans 12:2

Dear friends, do not be surprised at the painful trial you are suffering, as though something strange were happening to you. But rejoice that you participate in the sufferings of Christ, so that you may be overjoyed when his glory is revealed.

1 Peter 4:12–13

Many, O LORD my God,
*   are the wonders you have done.*
The things you planned for us
*   no one can recount to you;*
were I to speak and tell of them,
*   they would be too many to declare.*

Psalm 40:5

At Inspirio, we'd love to hear
your stories and your feedback.
Please send your comments to us
by way of email at
icares@zondervan.com